ABOUT THE AUTHOR
Dr. EddieVuittonet

Vuittonet has served as a self-defense instructor, graphic department director, sound technician, video CGI tech, computer technician, special investigator, job counselor, federal agent, collection agent, CEO of corporations, and part-time after-school assistant administrator for Agri-Business Management, Inc. (ABMI).

He is a certified graphic/audio/video artist and virtual assistant.

Vuittonet is a commercial artist, illustrator, 3D designer, videographer, 3D character animation creator/producer, and collectible pin button designer and maker.

He is a published author, ghostwriter, and copywriter of over 50 eBooks and manuals.

Vuittonet opened the first martial arts school in Raymondville, Texas, in 1971 and another in Harlingen, Texas.

By 1974, martial arts had led him to California.

He founded and taught self-defense techniques from different martial arts styles, known as Muryo Waza.

Vuittonet taught Muryo Waza at the Sal Mosqueda Community Center and a women's aerobic exercise class in Calwa, California.

Vuittonet and Sinchi Mike Akens re-created the five systems in the History of Rumi Maki with the help of two elders from the Peruvian community and three martial arts experts from the Muryo Waza training lineage.

He studied the TAKANAKUY, the fighting festivals of Peru, investigating the various punching, blocking, and kicking techniques.

Vuittonet guided Akens in forming the Muryo Waza - Luminous Warriors Alliance.

Vuittonet worked as a Community Development Specialist and Professional Karate/Kung Fu Instructor for the City of Fresno.

He recruited and encouraged students to join traditional and non-traditional youth development groups that he formulated, including the Bug Club, the Millionaire Club, and many Karate-Kung-Fu demonstration teams, especially as part of the City of Fresno's Community Development program.

He provided guidance and spiritual counseling to neighborhood youth and gang members.

Vuittonet, Joseph Fisher, and Antoinette, his deceased wife, created and chartered Boy Scout Troop 97 and Cub Scout Pack 97, which consisted of underprivileged blacks and Hispanic inner-city youth.

During a short hiatus from the City of Fresno job in 1976, Vuittonet and two of his Black Belt opened a martial arts school in Eagle Pass, Texas, and one in Piedras Negras, Mexico.

Vuittonet started writing as a young man, creating social program projects for the City of Fresno in 1975.

He co-authored the "Four Miler" Program/Manual and the Graphitti Prevention Program for the Department of Housing and Community Development, chiefly funded by the Community Development Block Grant Act of 1973.

Soon after, Vuittonet began authoring manuals and instruction books for various civic organizations.

In 1977, Vuittonet became an international bounty hunter in Mexico, a deputy constable, and ran Maverick Collections.

In 1978, he returned to teach for the City of Fresno. Also worked for the County of Fresno, the State of California, and Security Specialists Inc.

Vuittonet also opened The Comic Syndrome, a combination comic book shop, snack bar, and amusement game arcade.

In addition, he took part as a local director for Honda's mini-bike Nippum Project of 1979, the Four Miler program, and the Graffiti Prevention program.

In 1985, Vuittonet moved back to Texas to Vuittonet Ranch and opened a private investigation firm above city hall in Raymondville, Texas.

In 1985, Vuittonet renewed his Private Investigation license and developed several projects and ventures under the Investigations Security Observations Group (ISOG).

In 1988, Vuittonet worked for the County of Willacy as a Youth Counselor as part of the Job Training Partnership Act of 1982.

He also became a US Border Patrol Agent.
In 1995, Vuittonet registered numerous dot-com domain names and created, ran, and sponsored websites.

By 1998, he availed himself of Valley Telephone's DSL internet service and adjusted his internet business accordingly.

Vuittonet began creating websites and graphic art for business corporations.

Vuittonet also created E. and A. Productions, Eco-Tech Drilling, Vuittonet Feed & Seed, Early Bird Home Nursing, Inc., and Los Vecinos Adult Day Care, Inc.

Vuittonet rekindled his singing career as Eddie Vuittonet and the Time Travelers, a cover studio band.

Since 1978, he has marketed over 17 music albums and over 200 singles recorded.

Vuittonet was elected Justice of the Peace in 1989 and again in 2003.

Vuittonet returned his courtroom documents and officially resigned through the Willacy County Commissioners Court on January 1, 2004. Politics ensued.

By January 26, 2004, Vuittonet was advised he needed to resign from his position as the judge in Willacy County, Texas, after there was a complaint with the State Commission on Judicial Conduct containing allegations of judicial misconduct against him regarding his failure to comply with mandatory judicial, educational requirements for the fiscal year 2003.

In 2009, Vuittonet founded Madre Seca Films, First Prize Multi-Media Group, and Eddie Vuittonet Video Audio Studios.

He co-wrote *Twin 2 Movies* with Akens on behalf of Screen Play Productions (SSP) for Madre Seca Films LLC.

He released his first full-length animated movie called *We All Die Today*.

Since this release, based on a direct, exclusive sales market model, he developed the comic book version, which is scheduled for worldwide release in January 2023.

He is currently working on the sequel to ETAL - *The Skeletonzi*.

In 2019, he sustained a traumatic brain injury, which left him unable to walk, coupled with leukemia.

Vuittonet is working as a digital marketing graphic designer and videographer as part of the marketing agency aspect of Greatsolution4u.

He intends to help other businesses succeed by augmenting their promotional and advertisement efforts.
Currently, he is focused on inspirational, self-development eBooks, including a few biographical and genealogical ones.

Vuittonet is a publisher and franchise of the Muryo Waza TDP Fighting Science, a comprehensive eBook detailing technique and philosophical impetus of martial art style, essentially the summation of over fifty-five years of practicing and instructing the martial art style of Muryo Waza.

His 2nd movie is a work in progress.

Vuittonet has been featured on Fresno Radio stations, Fresno Bee newspaper, Eagle Pass, Texas, Piedras Negras, a Mexican newspaper, and Raymondville Chronicle in Willacy County.

"DROP THAT PHONE, AND YOU WON'T GET HURT"

(DO IT... DO IT NOW)

Dr. Eddie Vuittonet, Ph.D.

CHAPTER ONE: THE STRUGGLE

When you don't have your cell phone available, it's difficult to manage the feelings of separation that come with it.

Staying connected with friends and family can be hard, and staying on top of important tasks can take time and effort.

With your cell phone, it can be easier to stay in touch with people and it can be easier to stay organized.

It can also be hard to stay informed about what is happening in the world, and it's hard to stay up to date with the latest news and trends.

Connecting with friends and family can be easier with your cell phone.

You may need help to call or text them or even check in on social media.

You may need to catch up with their lives or know what is happening.

Phone separation can be especially difficult if you are close to them and rely on them for emotional support.

Connecting with them with your cell phone is easier, and staying in touch is hard.

With your cell phone, it can be easier to stay organized.

You may need help accessing important documents or remembering what tasks you need to do.

You may not keep track of your appointments or even remember when you need to be somewhere.

Phone separation can be especially difficult if you rely on your cell phone to stay organized and on top of your tasks.

Keeping informed about what is happening worldwide with your cell phone is easier.

You may not access the news or even know what is happening worldwide.

You may need help to stay updated with the latest trends or even know what is happening worldwide.

Phone separation can be especially difficult if you rely on your cell phone to stay informed and updated with the world.

With your cell phone, staying connected with people and staying organized can be easier.

It can also be difficult to stay informed about what is going on in the world.

Phone separation can be especially difficult if you rely on your cell phone to stay connected, organized, and informed.

It's hard to manage the feelings of separation that come with not having your cell phone available, but staying connected, organized, and informed is possible without it.

The struggle to put down the phone has become very difficult.

Most people work in front of a screen all day, and most do it at home too.

Numerous people go home after work, sit in front of the TV, and browse their phones.

Digitalization has become a way of life for us today.

Over 80% of the population owns a mobile device, and 57% have more than one type of device.

Our digital world is a simple escape from our reality and comes at a cost.

The impact on our brain, body, and behavior can significantly ruin relationships with people we love.

Not only are our electronic devices connected to the internet, but it is also in our car, the fridge, our watch, our games, and even our home.

As technology becomes omnipresent, how can we break free of digital addiction?

Here's a short survey to give you an idea of your relationship with technology.

CHAPTER TWO: THE DEPENDENCE SURVEY

While this is not a scientific survey, it gives you an idea of your relationship with the digital world.

1. How often do you check your cell phone?

2. How long do you spend on your cell phone each day?

3. Do you feel anxious if you don't have your cell phone?

4. Do you need to respond to messages and notifications immediately?

5. Do you need to connect to your cell phone constantly?

6. Do you need to check your cell phone even when you don't have any notifications?

7. Do you need to be always available to answer calls and messages?

8. Do you feel you must always keep your cell phone with you?

9. Do you feel you need to keep your cell phone on you even when sleeping?

10. Do you need to check your cell phone even when you're in the middle of doing something else?

11. Do you need to check your cell phone, even with friends or family?

12. Do you check your cell phone even when you're not expecting any notifications?

13. Do you need to check your cell phone even when you're in the middle of a conversation?

14. Do you feel like you need to check your cell phone even when you're in the middle of a task?

15. Do you feel like you need to check your cell phone even when you're in the middle of an activity? Do you sleep with your phone next to your bed?

16. Do you look at social media an hour or less before bed?

17. Is it hard to sit silently (ex: on your commute or in a car)?

18. Do you eat most of your meals in front of a screen?

19. Do you use your phone as an alarm?

20. Do you check social media while you are at work?

21. Do you usually check your phone as soon as there is a notification?

22. Do you turn on the TV when you come home from work?

23. Is your daily screen time more than 5 hours a day?

24. Is looking at your phone an automatic behavior you don't always do consciously?

25. How difficult is it for you to fall asleep or stay asleep?

26. Do you struggle with weight?

27. Do you have difficulty with your attention or concentration?

28. Do you check your phone or browse social media when you drive?

29. Do you sometimes feel like your phone vibrates, yet there are no notifications?

30. Do you feel anxious if you forget or haven't accessed your phone?

31. Do you find it irritating when people say you're not listening or paying attention to them while they speak to you?

32. Would you consider your electronic devices your most valuable belongings, something you could not live without?

33. Now calculate the totals; what do you notice?

Mostly NO: Great, that means that you have found a spot where you use devices, and they don't use you and admittedly don't govern your life.

Mostly YES: This is a sign that this guide is for you.

Your screen time influences your life; you might be losing a lot of time and energy on devices that don't fulfill you.

Besides, if you said "yes" to almost all the questions, you are likely an artist at escaping reality.

It might be time for you to take control of your life.

It won't be easy to unplug, but with determination and patience, you will get there!

Mostly I DON'T KNOW: This is not necessarily a good thing.

You might be in denial and unable to be aware of your behavior.

This guide will help you be more conscious of your habits and how you can live a more fulfilling life.

Whether you want to break up completely with social media or develop a healthier relationship with technology, the following five steps will help you positively change your behaviors.

CHAPTER THREE: WHAT FLOATS OUR BOAT

Our lives would be drastically different if we were not dependent on cell phones.

We have become so accustomed to always having our phones with us.

I can't imagine life without them.

Cellphones have become an integral part of our lives, and I can't imagine how our lives would be different if we were not so dependent on them.

First, our communication would be drastically different.

We rely heavily on cell phones for communication through text messages, phone calls, or social media.

With our cell phones, we can rely on more traditional methods of communication, such as letters, landlines, and face-to-face conversations.

If we were not so dependent on our cell phones, we would have to be more intentional about our communication, as it would take more effort and time to reach out to someone.

Second, our access to information would be limited.

We rely heavily on cell phones to access the internet and all the information it provides.

With cell phones, we can rely on more traditional methods of accessing information, such as books, newspapers, and magazines.

With cell phones, we would be more intentional about our research, as finding the needed information would take more effort and time.

Third, our entertainment would be limited.

We rely heavily on our cellphones for entertainment through streaming services, gaming, or social media.

Without our cellphones, we would have to rely on more traditional methods of entertainment, such as board games, books, and movies.

Finding something to do without cell phones would take more time and effort since we would have to be more intentional about our entertainment.

Fourth, our productivity would be affected.

We rely heavily on our cellphones for productivity, whether through productivity apps, calendar reminders, or task lists.

With our cell phones, we can rely on more traditional production methods, such as paper planners, notebooks, and sticky notes.

Because of the increased effort required to stay organized and on task with our cell phones, we must be more intentional about our productivity.

Finally, our social lives would be affected.

We rely heavily on our cellphones for social interaction, whether it be through text messages, phone calls, or social media.

Without our cellphones, we would have to rely on more traditional methods of social interaction, such as face-to-face conversations, letters, and phone calls.

Without cell phones, we would have to be more intentional about our social lives, as reaching out to someone would take more effort and time.

Our lives would be drastically different if we were not dependent on cell phones.

We would have to be more intentional about our communication, access to information, entertainment, productivity, and social lives.

With our cell phones, we can rely on more traditional methods, which would take more effort and time.

When we want to change our lives, we must identify a reason to help us sustain the change.

The best reasons are those close to our hearts instead of imposed by others.

You can identify your motivations by finding answers to the following question:

Why do I want to disconnect from the digital world?

What are the benefits of disconnecting from the digital world?

Write down all the reasons that come to mind.

Ensure you feel connected to personal reasons, such as "to have more energy and time with people I love," instead of extrinsic motivations like "because my partner or friends said so."

CHAPTER FOUR: ACCEPTING THE TRANSITION

Once you've listed your motivations, ask yourself:

On a scale of 1 to 10 (1 being not motivated, ten being highly motivated), how motivated are you to disconnect from the digital world?

Motivation matters in achieving success.

Staying motivated is difficult, especially when faced with obstacles or challenges.

However, it is possible to scale your motivation from one to ten.

Here are some tips to help you do just that.

First, set realistic goals.

It is important to set achievable goals that you can work towards.

This scaling process will help you stay motivated and focused on the task.

Second, break down your goals into smaller, more manageable tasks.

This scaling process will help you stay motivated and progress toward your goals.

Third, reward yourself for completing tasks.

This scaling process will help you stay motivated and give you a sense of accomplishment.

Fourth, stay organized.

Having a plan and a schedule will help you stay on track and be motivated.

Fifth, surround yourself with positive people.

Having positive people in your life will help you stay motivated and give you the support you need to reach your goals.

Sixth, stay focused. It is easy to get distracted, but staying focused on your goals is important.

Seventh, take breaks.

Taking breaks will help you stay motivated and give you time to recharge.

Eighth, stay motivated by reading inspiring stories. Reading stories of people who have succeeded will help you stay motivated and give you the courage to keep going.

Ninth, stay motivated by listening to motivational music.

Listening to music that inspires you will help you stay motivated and give you the energy to keep going.

Finally, stay motivated by believing in yourself.

Believe in yourself and your abilities; you can stay motivated and reach your goals.

If your score is under 5, there might be a better time for you.

You have an opportunity to reconsider your motivation and also the timing.

A score above 6 is likely to lead you to success.

If your answer was below 10, what would help you move one score higher?

In other words, what would make you more motivated to change?

What do you perceive as a benefit to disconnecting?

CHAPTER FIVE: COUNTING YOUR DIGITAL PANORAMA

Keeping track of your "screen time" is crucial for being aware of how much time you spend in front of a "digital panorama" and how much you want it to be be reduced.

Tracking your screen time is important in understanding how much time you spend in front of a digital panorama.

It can help you identify patterns and behaviors that you may not have noticed before, and it can help you set realistic goals to reduce your screen time.

The first step in tracking your screen time is to determine how much time you spend in front of a digital panorama daily.

You can count time spent on your computer, phone, tablet, or any other device with a screen.

You can use a timer or an app to track your screen time or keep a log of how much time you spend on each device.

Once you have determined how much time you spend in front of a digital panorama daily, you can set goals to reduce screen time.

Start by setting a goal of reducing screen time by a certain percentage each week.

As little as 10% or as much as 50% could be used.

Achieve a realistic and attainable goal.

Once you have set your goal, you can implement strategies to help you reach it.

Start by limiting the time you spend on each device.

For example, you could set a timer for yourself and only allow yourself to use your phone for a certain amount each day.

Limit the time you spend on social media or other websites.

Another strategy for reducing screen time is finding activities that don't involve a digital panorama.

Spend time with family and friends, take up a hobby, or go for a walk.

These activities can reduce screen time and help you stay connected with the people and things matter most.

Finally, it's important to know how much time you spend in front of a digital panorama and how much you wish to reduce it.

Tracking your screen time can help you identify patterns and behaviors that you may not have noticed before and can help you set realistic goals for reducing your screen time.

With a little effort and dedication, you can reduce your screen time and enjoy a healthier and more balanced lifestyle.

Adopting healthier behaviors requires increasing our awareness of technology use.

By controlling our screen time, we are more likely to change our habits and lives.

You can download an app that will calculate that for your phone and make sure to take note of screen time on other devices like TV or computers.

Your goal will be to see a reduction in screen time over the next weeks.

Every morning, you can note your screen time of the previous day and aim to reduce it.

CHAPTER SIX: PRACTICE MINDFULNESS

The next step is dedicated to actions.

Make a list of what you could do to help you reduce your time in the digital world.

Making a list of what you can do to help reduce your time in the digital world can be daunting.

It can take time to know where to start and how to make sure you are taking the right steps to reduce your digital time.

Here are some tips to help you get started.

1. Set a time limit for yourself.

Decide how much time you want to spend on digital devices daily and stick to it.

This process will help you stay focused and ensure you spend only a little time on digital activities.

2. Unplug from your devices.

Take a break from your devices and do something else.

This process could read a book, walking, or spending time with family and friends.

3. Limit notifications.

Turn off notifications from social media and other apps.

This process will help you stay focused and reduce your time on your devices.

4. Delete apps. Delete any apps that you don't use or don't need.

This process will help reduce the time you spend on your devices.

5. Use an app blocker.

Use an app blocker to limit the time you spend on certain apps.

This process will help you stay focused and reduce your time on your devices.

6. Take a digital detox.

Take a break from your devices and do something else.

Among these activities are reading a book, walking, or spending time with family and friends.

7. Set a bedtime. Set a bedtime for yourself and stick to it.

This process will help you get enough sleep and reduce your time on your devices.

Making a list of what you can do to help reduce your time in the digital world can be a great way to stay focused and reduce your time on your devices.

By following these tips, you can ensure you take the right steps to reduce your digital time.

Here are a few examples:

Practice Mindfulness.

Mindfulness doesn't have to be a complex meditation practice.

It can be a simple exercise of taking a moment to connect with your breath by taking three deep breaths.

Mindfulness is the act of observing our experience in the present moment.

Using the five senses is a great way to practice mindfulness.

Observe what you smell, see, hear, feel, or taste. Using your senses will bring you to the present moment.

CHAPTER SEVEN: NO MULTI-TASKING

In today's world, multitasking is often seen as a desirable skill.

People juggling multiple tasks at once are often seen as more productive and efficient.

However, there are many advantages to concentrating on one thing at a time.

When you focus on one task, you can give it your full attention.

Concentrating on one thing allows you to work more efficiently and effectively.

You can avoid distractions and stay on task.

You can also think more deeply and come up with better solutions.

By concentrating on one thing, you can also avoid making mistakes.

When you are multitasking, it is easy to become overwhelmed and make mistakes.

When you focus on one task, you can also save time.

Multitasking can be time-consuming, as you have to switch between tasks.

Concentrating on one thing can lead to a lot of wasted time.

When you focus on one task, you can complete it faster and move on to the next task.

Concentrating on one thing also allows you to be more creative.

When you multitask, thinking outside the box can be difficult.

When you focus on one task, you can explore different ideas and develop creative solutions.

Finally, concentrating on one thing can help you stay motivated.

When you multitask, staying focused and motivated cannot be easy.

When you focus on one task, you can stay motivated and complete the task.

Overall, there are many advantages to concentrating on one thing at a time.

It can help you work more efficiently and effectively, save time, be more creative, and stay motivated.

While multitasking can benefit some situations, it is important to remember the advantages of concentrating on one thing.

Our society tends to encourage multitasking.

On the other hand, it has created individuals who have difficulty being present.

If you spend time with a friend, be present, listen, and interact with the individual.

Turn off your notifications on your phone and keep eye contact with the person interacting with you.

CHAPTER EIGHT: PUT YOUR BRAIN THROUGH THE OBSTACLE COURSE

Putting your brain through a series of intuitive processes can increase mental agility and creativity.

Intuitive processes involve tapping into your subconscious mind to access information and ideas you may not have been aware of before.

This type of thinking can help you come up with new solutions to problems and can help you think more creatively.

The first step to putting your brain through intuitive processes is to relax.

Allow yourself to become calm and centered by taking a few deep breaths.

Relaxing will help you access the deeper parts of your mind and allow you to tap into your intuition.

Once you are relaxed, the next step is to focus on a particular problem or challenge that you are facing.

Spend some time thinking about the issue and developing possible solutions.

As you do this, allow yourself to be open to any ideas that come to mind.

Don't be afraid to explore different possibilities and to think outside the box.

The next step is to use visualization techniques to help you access your intuition.

Visualization involves creating a mental image of the problem or challenge and then allowing yourself to explore different solutions.

As you do this, pay attention to any feelings or sensations.

These can be clues to the answers that you are looking for.

The final step is to take action.

Once you have identified a potential solution, please take the steps to implement it.

Looking at your options could involve:

- Researching the issue further.
- Talking to people who may have more knowledge about it.
- Taking some action to move forward.

Putting your brain through a series of intuitive processes can greatly increase your mental agility and creativity.

It can help you come up with new solutions to problems and can help you think more creatively.

By taking the time to relax, focus on a particular problem or challenge, use visualization techniques, and take action, you can tap into your intuition and access the answers you seek.

It is possible to train your mind to focus on the present.

You can do so by recognizing when you think of the past or the future.

Choose a day or an hour when you will observe your thoughts.

During that time, catch yourself when you have thoughts connected to something outside the present moment, like thinking of what happened in your past or hoping for the future.

Once you catch yourself, take three deep breaths to return your attention to the present moment.

That way, you will get better at bringing your mind back to the present.

CHAPTER NINE: EAT WELL

Many people have learned to eat in front of the screen.

Unplugging while you eat allows you to be present and enjoy your food.

You force yourself to place your utensils on the table every bite you take and taste your food.

Observe the texture and the taste, and be mindful of every bite you take.

Eating at your desk in front of a computer or cell phone screen can be a convenient way to get a meal in during a busy day.

However, it can also be a habit that can lead to mindless eating and a lack of enjoyment of the food.

Eating in this way can lead to overeating, as well as a lack of appreciation for the food that you are consuming.

This chapter will discuss how you can enjoy your food more by not eating at your desk in front of a computer or cell phone screen.

The first step to enjoying your food more is to create a designated eating space.

This could be a separate room or area of your home, or even a spot outside.

This space should be free from distractions, such as computers, phones, and televisions.

This will help you focus on the food that you are eating and to appreciate the flavors and textures of the food.

A designated eating space will create a sense of ritual and routine around eating, making the experience more enjoyable.

The second step to enjoying your food more is to take the time to prepare the food.

This means taking the time to shop for ingredients, to plan out meals, and to cook the food.

Taking the time to prepare the food will help to create a sense of appreciation for the food that you are eating.

It creates a sense of satisfaction when you can create a delicious meal from scratch.

The third step to enjoying your food more is to take the time to sit down and eat.

This means taking the time to set the table, to serve the food, and to sit down and enjoy the meal.

Taking the time to sit down and eat will create a sense of mindfulness around the food that you are eating.

It will help to create a sense of appreciation for the food that you are consuming.

The fourth step to enjoying your food more is to take the time to savor the food.

This means taking the time to appreciate the flavors and textures of the food, as well as to appreciate the effort that went into preparing the meal.

Taking the time to savor the food will help to create a sense of appreciation for the food that you are eating.

It creates a sense of satisfaction when you are able to appreciate the flavors and textures of the food.

Finally, the fifth step to enjoying your food more is to take the time to talk and connect with the people that you are eating with.

This means taking the time to engage in conversation, to share stories, and to connect with the people that you are eating with.

Taking the time to talk and connect with the people that you are eating with will help to create a sense of appreciation for the food that you are eating.

It creates a sense of satisfaction when connecting with the people you eat with.

In conclusion, eating at your desk in front of a computer or cell phone screen can lead to mindless eating and a lack of enjoyment of the food.

If you make a special effort to create an eating area, prepare food, sit down and eat, savor the food, talk to the people you're eating with, and savor it, you'll be able to enjoy it more because you'll be able to spend more time enjoying your food.

Doing these things will help to create a sense of appreciation for the food you are eating and a sense of satisfaction when you can connect with the people you are eating with.

CHAPTER TEN: PROGRAM FOR SLEEP

Instead of scrolling through social media posts before bed, acknowledge what you are grateful for in the present.

List all the things that, at this moment, you are thankful for.

Gratitude is a powerful emotion that can have a profound effect on our lives.

It is an attitude of appreciation and thankfulness for our blessings.

We can express gratitude by simply saying "thank you" by writing a heartfelt letter of appreciation.

It is a way of acknowledging the good things in our lives and recognizing the people and circumstances that have helped us along the way.

The importance of gratitude cannot be overstated. It is a way of recognizing the abundance in our lives and the gifts we have been given.

It can help us appreciate the small things and focus on our lives positive aspects.

Gratitude can also help us cultivate a sense of contentment and joy, even amid difficult times.

When we focus on the things we are grateful for, we can become more mindful of our blessings and less likely to take them for granted.

Gratitude can help us appreciate life's beauty and savor the moments we have.

It can also help us cultivate a sense of optimism and hope, even in adversity.

Gratitude can also help us build stronger relationships with others.

When we express our appreciation for the people in our lives, we can create a deeper connection and foster a sense of trust and understanding.

Gratitude can also help us be more generous and compassionate towards others, as we recognize the importance of giving back to those who have given to us.

Gratitude can also help us become more resilient in the face of adversity.

When we focus on the things we are grateful for, we can become more aware of our strengths and resources and use them to cope with difficult situations.

Gratitude can also help us stay focused on our goals and to take action towards achieving them.

Finally, gratitude can help us cultivate inner peace and contentment.

When we focus on the things we are grateful for, we can become more mindful of the present moment and appreciate the beauty of life.

Gratitude can also help us cultivate a sense of joy and satisfaction, even amid difficult times.

In conclusion, gratitude is an important emotion that can profoundly affect our lives.

It can help us appreciate the small things and focus on our lives positive aspects.

It can also help us build stronger relationships and be more resilient in adversity.

Finally, gratitude can help us cultivate inner peace and contentment.

By fixating on all the things and blessings we should be grateful for, we can create a life of abundance and joy.

CHAPTER ELEVEN: REST

Many people do not have limits or boundaries regarding social media.

Setting healthy boundaries is essential to improving our relationship with Facebook or Instagram.

You can do so by identifying a specific time when

you are offline when you believe it is best not to look at social media.

For example, you could decide that the first two hours of your day are offline.

That way, you don't have to let social media influence your mood that day.

It may take some days to adapt, and remember; research says that it takes 21 days to form a habit.

CHAPTER TWELVE: DROP THE PHONE

Put Your Phone Aside.

When interacting with others, whether at a family dinner or hanging out with friends, make a point to put your phone away.

Social Media can quickly pull you into a rabbit hole where you will completely forget your surroundings and realize that you are not enjoying the present moment with people in your circle.

Putting your phone aside will increase the quality of interaction you have with others and also bring more enjoyment.

CHAPTER THIRTEEN: FIGURE OUT WHAT YOU LIKE ON SOCIAL MEDIA

The incredible roller coaster of emotions that social media can lead you to:

Take the time to be aware of how you feel when you see or read a post.

Make a point to "unfollow" any individuals that make you feel bad.

Choosing what you want to see on social media is an important decision that could improve your relationship with it.

In the age of social media, it is becoming increasingly important to create and maintain healthy time-oriented boundaries in order to improve our relationships with people on Facebook or Instagram.

Social media has become an integral part of our lives, and it is important to understand how to use it in a healthy and productive way.

This essay will explore how creating and maintaining healthy time-oriented boundaries can help to improve our relationships with people on Facebook or Instagram.

It will discuss the importance of setting boundaries, the benefits of doing so, and the potential pitfalls of not setting boundaries.

The Importance of Setting Boundaries The first step in creating and maintaining healthy time-oriented boundaries is to understand the importance of setting boundaries.

Boundaries are important because they help to define the limits of our relationships with others.

They help to ensure that our relationships remain healthy and respectful, and that our interactions are mutually beneficial.

Boundaries also help to protect us from being taken advantage of or manipulated by others.

Setting boundaries is also important because it allows us to prioritize our own needs and wants.

It allows us to focus on our own goals and interests, rather than those of others.

This helps to ensure that we are not sacrificing our own needs and wants in order to please others.

Benefits of Setting Boundaries Once we understand the importance of setting boundaries, we can explore the benefits of doing so.

Setting boundaries can improve our relationships with people on Facebook or Instagram in several ways.

First, setting boundaries can help to ensure that our interactions with others are respectful and mutually beneficial.

By setting boundaries, we can ensure that our interactions are not one-sided or manipulative.

This helps to create a more positive and respectful environment for our interactions.

Second, setting boundaries can help to protect us from being taken advantage of or manipulated by others.

By setting boundaries, we can ensure that our interactions are not one-sided or manipulative.

This helps to create a more positive and respectful environment for our interactions.

Finally, setting boundaries can help to ensure that our interactions are meaningful and productive.

By setting boundaries, we can ensure that our interactions are focused on meaningful topics and activities, rather than simply wasting time.

This helps to create a more productive and enjoyable environment for our interactions.

Potential Pitfalls of Not Setting Boundaries While setting boundaries can be beneficial, it is also important to understand the potential pitfalls of not setting boundaries.

Not setting boundaries can lead to several negative outcomes, including:

1. Unhealthy relationships: Without boundaries, our relationships can become unhealthy and one-sided.

This can lead to feelings of resentment and frustration, and can ultimately damage our relationships with others.

2. Manipulation: Without boundaries, we can become vulnerable to manipulation by others. This can lead to us feeling taken advantage of, and can ultimately damage our relationships with others.

3. Wasted time: Our interactions can become unfocused and unproductive without boundaries.

This can lead to us wasting time on activities that could be more meaningful and beneficial.

Conclusion In conclusion, creating and maintaining healthy time-oriented boundaries is essential to improving our relationships with people on Facebook or Instagram.

Setting boundaries helps to ensure that our interactions are respectful and mutually beneficial, and that our interactions are meaningful and productive.

Not setting boundaries can lead to several negative outcomes, including unhealthy relationships, manipulation, and wasted time.

For these reasons, it is important to understand the importance of setting boundaries, and to create and maintain healthy time-oriented boundaries in order to improve our relationships with people on Facebook or Instagram.

CHAPTER FOURTEEN: KEEP YOUR EMOTIONS IN CHECK

Practicing emotional awareness means paying attention to your emotions while watching social media.

Every time you catch yourself feeling down.

Take a screen time timeout of one minute.

During that minute, focus on your breathing.

Take six deep breaths every time you have a negative emotion.

The key to success is to identify realistic and practical ways for you.

There is no need to take an all-or-nothing approach. Reducing your time in front of a screen will make you more comfortable with reality.

In the modern world, social media has become an integral part of our lives.

We use it to stay connected with our friends and family, to share our thoughts and feelings, and to keep up with the latest news and trends.

However, it is important to remember that social media can also be a source of stress and anxiety if we don't take steps to create and maintain healthy emotional boundaries and interactions with people on Facebook or Instagram.

In this chapter, I will delineate the importance of creating and maintaining healthy emotional boundaries and interactions with people on social media and provide some tips on how to do so.

The Importance of Healthy Emotional Boundaries and Interactions Creating and maintaining healthy emotional boundaries and interactions with people on social media is essential for our mental health and wellbeing.

It is important to remember that social media is a public platform, and that anyone can see our posts and interactions.

This means that it is important to be mindful of what we post and how we interact with others.

It is also important to remember that our posts and interactions can have a lasting impact on our relationships with others, both online and offline.

Creating healthy emotional boundaries and interactions with people on social media can help us protect our mental health and wellbeing.

It can help us avoid negative interactions with others, such as cyberbullying or trolling.

It can also help us avoid becoming overwhelmed by the information we are exposed to on social media.

Tips for Creating and Maintaining Healthy Emotional Boundaries and Interactions:

We can take several steps to create and maintain healthy emotional boundaries and interactions with people on social media.

1. Set Boundaries: It is important to set boundaries for yourself when it comes to social media.

This means deciding what types of posts and interactions you are comfortable with, and setting limits on how much time you spend on social media.

2. Be Mindful of What You Post: It is important to be mindful of what you post on social media.

This means avoiding posting anything that could be seen as offensive or hurtful to others.

3. Avoid Engaging in Negative Interactions: It is important to avoid engaging in negative interactions with others on social media.

This means avoiding engaging in cyberbullying or trolling and instead focusing on positive interactions.

4. Take Breaks: It is important to take breaks from social media to avoid becoming overwhelmed.

By taking time away from social media, you can focus on other activities and give yourself a break from constantly being bombarded with information.

In conclusion, it is important to remember that creating and maintaining healthy emotional boundaries and interactions with people on social media is essential for our mental health and wellbeing.

By setting boundaries, being mindful of what we post, avoiding engaging in negative interactions, and taking breaks from social media, we can ensure that our social media use is beneficial to our mental health and wellbeing.

CHAPTER FIFTEEN: CREATE AN ITINERARY SCHEDULE

It is time to implement all the actions you've identified in chapter 4.

Choose a day this week when you will apply your first action.

That day will begin your journey to take back control of your devices.

Once you've chosen a date, pick your action!

Awareness and transferring your activities to be more offline than in front of the screen can improve your well• being.

Being offline also increases your sense of living in the present moment.

Experiencing your reality can be more rewarding than the digital world.

To maintain a healthy relationship with technology, we must find a balance.

Being in control means that technology is not using you.

Spend less time and energy on social media.

It is recommended to monitor your screen time; awareness will be essential to maintain a balanced and healthy relationship with technology.

Not only will you be able to regain a fulfilling life, but you will also set an excellent example for others to follow.

.

Creating and maintaining a daily and weekly planner cannot be overstated.

A well-structured planner can help you stay organized, on top of tasks, and productive.

It can also help you avoid distractions, such as social media, that can detract from your productivity.

In this chapter, I will discuss the importance of creating and maintaining a daily and weekly planner that does not involve any allowance for going to social media for entertainment or social stimulation.

First, it is important to understand why it is important to create and maintain a daily and weekly planner.

A planner can help you stay organized and on top of tasks.

It can also help you prioritize tasks and set goals.

By having a plan, you can ensure that you are focusing on the most important tasks and not wasting time on unnecessary activities.

A planner can help you stay focused and motivated.

It can also help you stay on track and avoid procrastination.

When creating and maintaining a daily and weekly planner, it is important to ensure that it does not involve any allowance for going to social media for entertainment or social stimulation.

Social media can be a major distraction and can take away from your productivity.

Limiting your time on social media can be difficult, so it is best to avoid it altogether. When creating and maintaining a daily and weekly planner, it is important to ensure it is realistic and achievable.

Set realistic goals and tasks that you can accomplish.

It is important to make sure that you are staying focused on tasks.

Giving yourself enough time to complete tasks is important rather than setting yourself up for failure.

It is also important to make sure that you are taking breaks throughout the day.

Breaks are important for your mental and physical health.

Taking breaks can help you to stay focused and productive.

It can help you avoid burnout and fatigue. Finally, it is important to make sure that you are setting aside time for yourself.

It is important to make sure that you are taking care of yourself and that you are not neglecting your own needs.

Taking time for yourself can help you stay focused and productive.

It can help you avoid burnout and fatigue.

In conclusion, creating and maintaining a daily and weekly planner that does not involve any allowance for going to social media for entertainment or social stimulation is important.

A well-structured planner can help you stay organized, on top of tasks, and productive.

It can help you avoid distractions like social media that can detract from your productivity.

It is important to make sure that your planner is realistic and achievable, that you are taking breaks throughout the day, and that you are setting aside time for yourself.

www.ingramcontent.com/pod-product-compliance
Lightning Source LLC
Chambersburg PA
CBHW081454220526
45466CB00008B/2638